The Town of Insomniacs

poems by

Rosetta Marantz Cohen

Finishing Line Press
Georgetown, Kentucky

The Town of Insomniacs

Copyright © 2018 by Rosetta Marantz Cohen
ISBN 978-1-63534-802-6 First Edition
All rights reserved under International and Pan-American Copyright Conventions. No part of this book may be reproduced in any manner whatsoever without written permission from the publisher, except in the case of brief quotations embodied in critical articles and reviews.

ACKNOWLEDGMENTS

Poems have previously appeared in the following journals:

The Town of Insomniacs (*Carolina Quarterly*)
Word Problems, There were six of us at dinner (*Feminist Quarterly*)
The Philosopher Puts up a Fence (*The Drexel Online Journal*)
Children and Facts (*Denver Quarterly*)
Repair, Elegy (*Spirit*)

Publisher: Leah Maines
Editor: Christen Kincaid
Cover Art: Rosetta Marantz Cohen
Author Photo: Jon Crispin, courtesy of Louise W. and Edmund J. Kahn Liberal Arts Institute, Smith College
Cover Design: Leah Huete

Printed in the USA on acid-free paper.
Order online: www.finishinglinepress.com
also available on amazon.com

Author inquiries and mail orders:
Finishing Line Press
P. O. Box 1626
Georgetown, Kentucky 40324
U. S. A.

Table of Contents

Word Problems 1

Grandma's Bedroom, Brooklyn 3

Depression Quilt 4

The Town of Insomniacs 5

Kitchen Sink 6

Invisible Labor 7

Family 8

There were six of us at dinner 10

Gifts from Foreigners 12

Land Grant School 13

The Philosopher Puts Up a Fence 14

The Famous Poet (and Son) Pays a Visit 15

Children and Facts 16

The Kiss 17

My Millennial 18

Repair 19

Elegy 20

Frequent Flyer 21

Astronaut 22

Fairytale 23

For Sam, as always

Word Problems

The heat of father's flannelled knee
against my own obsesses me,

and how his callused fingers look
pressing against the opened book.

"Listen," he says, and reads as one
might read aloud to a simpleton:

"A speeding train departs at eight;
figure the distance and the rate."

My father holds a secret key
that could unlock this mystery,

but through my own uncertain stealth
I must discover it myself.

"Figure it out," he says, and then,
"For heaven's sake, at least begin!"

Up on the mantel grandma's face
looks down behind a wall of glass,

and mother turns, as in a dream,
the pages of a magazine.

I hear the cruel kitchen clock
contemptuously tick and tock.

"Help me." I try to make my voice
bend down before my father's face

already dark with reprimand:
"You never try to understand,"

he says, and then he reads again,
but louder now, "A speeding train..."

A speeding train departs at eight,
departs at eight from the darkened gate

and the soldier lights his cigarette
and thinks of a woman he has met

in another town, and the hands of fate
that impose this distance, (which is great)

and this rate of loss (a terrible rate).
"Hurry," says father, "it's getting late..."

But anything now that I might say
wouldn't solve the problem anyway.

Grandma's Bedroom, Brooklyn

Two twin beds stand neatly side by side
Like an Amish farmer and his bride.

Hair pins sit beside a silver globe
On a shelf of the opened chifferobe

And on the nightstand, on a sterling tray,
A sterling hairbrush, burnishing to gray

Holds a knot of gray and yellow hair
Scented of talcum and of lavender.

Grandfather's black boots, polished every night,
Seem to consume and not reflect the light,

As they sit, like dark boats on a polished shore,
Filled with the shadows of the Great War.

Light-flecked dust hangs in the still air,
Marking the distance between here and there.

Depression Quilt

A sky, a road, a cleft of muslin cloud;
A wire fence, a low deserted barn;
A house with windows, bright as yellow yarn,
That cast no light. Pale fields, unplowed,

Stretch into barren flats of beige and brown;
And all the shadows trees no longer cast
Settle like sun-bleached pages of a past
That heat and silence serve to fasten down.

Thread through the dusty yard with your empty bags.
We welcome any guest to our kitchen door,
And feed him from the larder of the poor,
And bid him rest all night on a bed of rags.

The Town of Insomniacs

We have all of us begun to dream on our feet.
Out of nowhere, the cobbler, raising his club to a sole,
Will think of a garden, a woman, anything—
And his hand unclasps, the leather drops to the floor;
You can hear him sigh, then fall into even breaths
That is something but not the same
As the sound of sleep.

What will become of us, laboring all night,
Desperate for work, a floor to sweep?
Nothing is left untended. The house shines.
The children demand more chores; the cattle
Grow slow and confused, brought to the fields at all hours
To cut trails under the moon.
Horses are beaten for their lassitude
And then, when the roads block up with carcasses,
We are glad for the task of burying the dead.

What will become of us?
The skins of our palms grow hard as hooves;
The skins of our backs like hide
From the friction of clothes.
Will we lose the sense of words:
What the dawn does?
Why the swamp crane closes its eyes
When the sky turns dark?
Will our own eyes atrophy until
The iris hardly remembers the warmth of a lid;
And children are told the fable of a time
When men lay down for hours
And forgot themselves?

Kitchen Sink

How long has it taken into itself
The ravages of human appetite; colluded
In waste, in cover-up; become
An instrument of forgetting?
Along its porcelain flanks
Whole armies of innocents have passed,
Funneled into darkness. What it knows
Of the habits and the hearts of men
Emerges uncensored daily from our lips:
Dull argument or stridency or nag,
The small ones' angry fists against the chairs;
Sometimes a brief kindness or a laugh.
But soon, again, the brutal ritual,
The scraped plates heaped against its chest,
The water blast, the unforgiving sponge.
Then finally the fearsome jaws take in
To themselves the sink's unfinished work,
and strip away all remnants of the past.
Tomorrow, when we use the plates again,
It will be as if the past had never been.

Invisible Labor

Because I cannot control it, the sun rises.
And because I have no say in the matter, I
Place the key in the slip of lock that someone invented
After great, solitary labor,
And drive to work on roads that hold my body over their black surface,
A surface of hard macadam
That others once shoveled and smoothed.
Because I am powerless to change it,
I arrive at work, the building
Pulling me into its darkness;
The cool finality of arrival itself a road
That others labored to create:
The system that defines my tasks,
That computes my worth,
That moves my limbs and mouth
To ordained completion.
What weariness at the day's end,
Freighted with all I am compelled to do
By virtue of secret doctrines!
The bed I rest on groans
From the weight of its making;
The sheets from the great machines
That snap and sting them into being,
As my body in space disrupts the static
Of air; air itself being an intrusion
On space, laboring to prevail
Over emptiness.

Family

Ned likes baroque music. He plays
It when the baby is falling asleep,
Thinking about his years of study
And the rigors of mastering his instrument,
Which he has necessarily put aside now
For more remunerative work.

Brilliant Cora likes birds, likes needlework,
Likes to sing as she plays
With the baby. This new idleness is fine now,
An opportunity to enjoy motherhood, to sleep
And read. Why should she be an instrument
Of commerce, she thinks, lounging now in the study

Beside Olivia, her sweet firstborn, a study
In pink, a true girl, assiduously at work
On some imaginary project; Cora could watch her play
For hours, her little hands fretting the rug like an instrument,
Then staring wordlessly into the distance, now
As quiet as if she were asleep.

Is it normal for a wakened child to seem asleep?
To have no inclination to talk or study?
And she, Cora, what has she become now,
So far removed from meaningful work,
A mere minor character in a play,
A mere maternal instrument?

Ned thinks of himself as an instrument-
alist: Logic requires he work, eat, sleep;
If once he had time to dream to play,
If once he could indulge his love of study,
Now, his youth gone, it is time for work.
Pleasure, he thinks, has no meaning now;

Just the tedium of family life. Now
The dreaded Cora, that dull instrument,
Calls him to help her with some domestic work,
Some dull task, and he will rise and help her, sleep-
Walking, as usual, through the day; play-
Acting at fatherhood, a study

In misery. The baby never sleeps now. Never;
Her cry an instrument of torture. Strange ideas play in his head:
Do others find love requires such arduous work, such endless study?

There were six of us at dinner

There were six of us at dinner:
Partnered for life, three women and three men.
We were staid, civilized, three women
And three men, all of a certain age.
Having weathered the worst and best
Of life; we had, in a sense, arrived.

It was late. We had all of us arrived
At that comfortable place after dinner
When we suspected that this was the best
Our lives would ever be. Men
Spoke about their teams, their stocks; women
About clothes, the indignities of age.

One said, "I have finally reached the age
when I am invisible to men; arrived
at a place where I am, in a sense, post-woman."
There was silence then, among us women at dinner.
"…And I'm glad of it," she said, "to be free of men's
Sexual assessment. In school, I was always the best

In my class, straight A's, but the best
Thing about me, I always knew, was my age
And my beauty. I knew my professors, all men,
Saw only this when I would arrive
At their office hours. Or over dinner,
Later, with male clients—my sexual power as a woman."

And then the second of us spoke, the second woman:
"I called it 'flattery' in those days," she said, "Putting the best
Face on what was harassment; dinners
That ended in groped kisses from men twice my age."
And then I told them about the teacher who arrived
At my door at night, drunk, saying "I'm a man;

What do you expect?" How I had felt man-
ipulated and ashamed, and had never told another woman,
even though I knew the same man arrived
at other doors asking the same question. Perhaps it was best,
we said, that we had kept these secrets. It was another age;
we still ended up here after all: happy, among friends at dinner.

We studied our husbands as they spoke: good men,
Certainly; middle-aged fathers of daughters; and wondered
If other women were right now speaking about them at dinner.

Gifts from Foreigners

A wooden cup. A doll whose linen dress
Smells of the sun-baked marketplace
Of Istanbul or Marrakesh or Thrace.
A pillow, small and functionless.

Also: a string of beaded yellow clay
Which like the polyester square
Of printed fabric I will never wear,
But cannot bring myself to give away.

Their faces gone. Their voices, like the sea,
Blend into breaking sounds that sound the same.
Only these odd and useless things remain,
Like a moral scold or a homily.

Land Grant School

The speaker was talking about the novel, how today
Ecocriticism relies on too narrow a canon,
When suddenly, as if seized by an idea, the man on
The stage in the large auditorium turned away

From his notes to ask the audience of students,
"How many here have ever milked a cow?"
To which the erstwhile silent uttered: "wow"
collectively, and roused themselves, feeling a sense

That something strange and wonderful was here;
That plowing through this barren exegesis,
One may unearth a nugget of mimesis—
The moo of meaning suddenly made clear.

200 hands go up, slicing the air like sickles:
"Raised it, milked it, watched it go to slaughter!"
"Huh!" said the speaker, taking a sip of water,
Then turning back to an essay by Ashton Nichols.

The Philosopher Puts up a Fence

Several age-old conundrums assert themselves
as you trot behind Bob of Bob's Fences,
marking the way his trowel on the soil
parses the yard in two: 1) the senses

and the intellect are at odds here;
the senses bristle at the imposition of order
(not to mention the sheer ugliness of the fence)…
but the mind (or *your* mind) loves a border,

a concept framed; a text contextualized
(as your first book on "mind frames" demonstrated).
Amid the irrational, the ambiguous, the continuing
absence of a unified theory, a gated

fence ensures a certain certainty, while keeping
the dog away from the herb garden. Still, 2)
what are you fencing in and fencing out?
What are the consequences? You who

wrote on "community" as a categorical imperative,
must mark above Bob's shoulder now the face
of your own palpable and often annoying neighbor,
scowling at her sill. If only you could replace

her with the *idea* of a neighbor…(or for that matter,
the fence with the idea of a fence), you could walk
your hypothetical dog in the vast and interesting
verdure of your mind, fenced where reason dictates fences work,

open where openness makes greatest sense,
forgetting problems both ineffable and concrete:
(the mistakenly thawed eggs at the fertility clinic, etc.)
feeling the fact of the earth beneath your feet;

or like the great stoics, pacing the marble porches
of temples, inventing the State, debating the idea of The Good,
you too might walk the clear geometry of the yard,
inventing and reinventing the neighborhood.

The Famous Poet (and Son) Pays a Visit

Pale as the floral print of the host's settee,
you sit, remote, a fragile drooping flower;
while at your feet the tweedy pageantry
of your idolators ignore you passionately,
or try to match your grimace, dour for dour.
Back in the early days when your first book
Was called "ecstatic" by the TLS,
you'd liked this sort of thing:
Some poetess, sprawled like an odalisque in a fauteuil,
could spark inspired visions of undress.
Your mind was fecund then; how effortless
were metaphors for every kind of joy!
Now it is different. Everything's the same.
The piquancy is gone. You say, *I guess
With age we lose some pleasure in the game;*
or so it seems now when some poetess,
leaning seductively in towards your better ear,
inquires after your wife by her first name.
You sip your Coke pretending not to hear,
until at last your son says, "Mom is fine,"
shrugging (but subtly) at you with disdain.
Soon you will plead "a fever," slip to the street,
leaning against this Telemachus, you
will think of the grasses smothered underfoot,
the tiny birds that peck at the sewer grate;
will wind with him past storefronts dimly lit,
(*"Like faces from which all the life is drained"*)
then back to the borrowed flat of a renowned
colleague, where you'll drink his gin
till dawn, and write the same poem again.

Children and Facts

There is something poignant in their love of them,
the way they hold a cool fact up to the light
and run their little fingers over its surface.
For them the bleak winter of the Pilgrims
conflates to a dense and tangible fact,
like something freeze-dried,
tart with a porous potential;
and all the Olympian gods line up in a row
ready to yield their power; dates,
names, battles lost and won, all
swallowed in their pure form; swallowed whole,
and born again, out of the head, like Athena.

How fast that talent ebbs in puberty!
The mind, grown thick with subtlety and desire,
gropes its way towards facts, and finds at the summit
little of pleasure—"What is the point of this?"
The question, never asked in childhood,
now blunts the fact's first force, and then,
under the weight of abstraction, blots it out.

The Kiss

"Kiss me," I say to Liz; at almost two,
her lips are cool and pink and petal-new.
So nodding to a tongue she barely speaks,
She lays her little hands against my cheeks,
And shows me with a kiss she understands
The vagaries of parental demands.

My little darling, will you still embrace
With so much tenderness your mother's face
When she's grown very old and full of need?
Already in your dark eyes I can read
Some future daughter, dutiful, whose kiss
Hardly betrays its own distractedness.

My Millennial

What you call *home*—
Cat-pungent and damp as a sponge, cluttered
With flyers for freegan lectures, hot yoga—
Mocks home, mocks comfort and the myths of childhood.
Irony dents the den's Formica floor;
Anxiety, the stolid certitudes of the six o'clock meal.

Here is your American Dream: tributaries of desire leading
Into a great sea of justice, where you and your kind
Are liberated from me and my kind, and the poor are less poor,
And the rich, ashamed of themselves, retreat into peaceful,
Compulsive philanthropy. Beautiful dream,
Where poetry sings from the rafters in multiple languages.

You take on the cast of your time, there's no opting out;
Swimming in the molecules of the day, bound by the digital
Human, slave-wage-interned tourniquet
Of the present. Poor girl:
When your media class ends, call me
And I will tell you again the way it all works out.

Repair

Nothing repairs so poorly as a toy.
No cracked doll returned from mending
ever resembles itself new,
first flung from the box
amid paper and tissue.

Shoes, too, rehabilitate
like former convicts, shiny in the extreme;
replaced soles, replaced lasts,
but still the fact of *use*
eludes the cobbler's art.

Or friendship, once rent,
never gets un-rent.
Despite passionate retractions
the cruel word thickens in the wound
like a missed staple.

Mourning is a kind of poor repair:
distractions and platitudes,
friends' voices, the rabbi's
elliptical drone
stitch and suture,
but under the banded gash
permanently lurks the diminishment.

Elegy

One by one they start to drift away,
the friends we thought we'd love eternally;
not through anger, not through argument,
but gradually, discretely, over time,
as if time were itself an argument
that neither stubborn party could resolve.

Now that friend, to whom you once confessed
the darkest secrets of you heart and soul,
is stranger even than the man who comes,
with lowered eyes, to sweep the vestibule.

So even as we speak, without our knowing,
many we think we love are moving too
out of our hearts. It is as if our hearts
were beating out the anthem of their going.

Frequent Flyer

Where the good and bad sit randomly
like playing cards in a deck, suspended
over the green felt table of the Midwest,
truths rise up in unexpected ways.

Once, between a structural engineer
and the Bridgeport postmaster,
we discussed the importance of prayer;
once, with an ex-marine, the supreme value of friendship.

Men, one often finds, are kinder
in the air; their stained ties falling
between splayed knees as they reach down
to retrieve a protein bar or offer to share their USA Todays.

Someone who owns a guardrail company
once fixed my laptop over Schenectady;
and someone who designs board games
ranked for me the best eastern casinos.

Among clouds, the distilled
lives of the world emerge and coalesce;
their essences condensed to one potent dose;
each, a short poem, read once and remembered.

Astronaut

In space, my body is one among other bodies: planets, stars
of unknown properties; perhaps others, like me,
contain water, contain flesh; rock and human,
Gas and light, all bending to the same laws of gravity.

On earth, it is more complex. I miss
the barked commands of the radio; the benign,
patriarchal culture of Mission Control:
their status reports on the hour,
their monitors gauging my heart
to the barest inflection. Here, worlds collide
and nobody flinches. Someone devastates a child,
someone destroys a family, and not even static
records itself on a screen. I fell

out of love with my husband and into love
with somebody else: When they test you
for stamina, for courage, for fortitude,
they don't test you for blind passion; after all,
love has no proper function in outer space,
and what we build and destroy beyond the world
demands neither conscience nor loyalty;

there being so much emptiness there,
so little chance of creating significant damage.

Fairytale

Prince, castle with a thousand rooms, and moat
I have, and servants and a thousand, thousand subjects,
All who love me for the good I've done,
Hold pageants for me, write me into myths.
By him—strong, attuned, a kind of Pericles—
I have the rarest child: almost not human
In her loveliness, and blessed
With the lithe grace of an animal…
Never was a girl so much rewarded
For having an imagination; for preferring
The hideous to the familiar;
The dark tower, locked door, strange master.
Much I received for being just myself. Now I am older.
The bards are busy with themes of love and death;
Love thwarted, love between men and gods,
And the world, it seems, is endlessly at peace
Since from abroad each day comes only weather—
Cloudless, blue, insistent temperateness.
Out in the garden, roses bloom and bloom.
I tend them for their thorns, and watch the hills
For some foreshadow of a shift in plot.

Rosetta Marantz Cohen is Myra M. Sampson Professor of Education and Faculty Director of the Lewis Global Studies Center at Smith College. She received a BA in English from Yale University, an MFA from Columbia University and an Ed.D. from Teachers College, Columbia.

Her previous chapbook (*Domestic Scenes*) was chosen my Maxine Kumin as winner of the Poets of the Foothills International Chapbook Competition. She is the author of five books on educational history and policy, including most recently, *The Work and Lives of Teachers: A Global Perspective* (Cambridge University Press, 2017). She lives in Northampton, MA with her husband, Sam Scheer.

www.ingramcontent.com/pod-product-compliance
Lightning Source LLC
LaVergne TN
LVHW041520070426
835507LV00012B/1715